Between Fear and Hope

the discipline of integration

Nick Aridas

FOREWORD

Losing your job suddenly at 55 leaves you with something confronting and unexpected:

Time.

Time fuelled by urgency. A sense that you should be doing something... anything... productive.

I have never been one to sit still.

So, it took real effort to sit still long enough to recognise the opportunity in front of me:

To finally keep a promise I had made to my younger self more than thirty years ago - that one day, I would write something that mattered.

And it is important that we keep our promises.
Especially the ones we make to ourselves.

So, I began with what felt most important: letters to my loved ones, written to be read after I was gone.

That is how this book began.

As deeply personal letters to my wife, my sons, and to future grandchildren I may never meet.

When I first shared them with my wife, she asked whether I
was truly comfortable revealing such intimate parts of our
lives to the world.

She was right.

Some things are too personal to publish exactly as they
were written.

So, the work evolved.

What began as private letters became something broader:

Letters to all those who shaped me - my ancestors, my
parents, my loves, my losses, my fears, and my hopes.

The original letters to my wife and sons remain, for now,
where they belong.

Perhaps one day.

Until then, this is the more universal version.

I have tried to be as honest and authentic as this work
allows. A book written in the tradition of my ancestors -
not merely to be read, but to be spoken, sung, wrestled
with, and argued over.

I hope something within it speaks to you.

Sincerely,
Nick

For my beloved,
who believed in me,
even when I no longer did.

For my sons,
who gave me the purpose needed.

For everyone who shaped me.

And for the promise
I made to myself.

LETTERS – what has shaped me

- To my Ancestors
- To my Parents
- To my Beloved
- To my Sons
- To my Friends
- To my Enemies
- To my Younger Self
- To my Inner Council

THE GROUND BETWEEN – how I have shaped my world

- Fear and Hope
- Reason and Intuition
- Power and Restraint
- Anger and Forgiveness
- Communication and Connection
- Freedom and Responsibility
- Systems that Serve and Systems that Devour
- Legacy and Continuity
- Knowledge and Wisdom
- Science and Spirituality

TO MY ANCESTORS

I was not born at the beginning.

I entered mid-story –
mid-storm,
mid-argument -
between forces older than memory.

Before me, men carved names into stone
and called it permanence.

Before me, other men burned those same stones and
called it progress.

I am the continuation of both –
the builders and the breakers.

Your hopes and fears.

Your unfinished works and your greatest triumphs.
Your victories sung.
Your death lamented.

You are not symbols or archetypes.

You are real - and alive in me.

Men and women negotiating survival
with the tools of your time.

Some of you built, some of you destroyed –
and some of you did both.

Some endured, some broke –
not from weakness, but from weight.

Some passed down voice.

Others, silence.

I have felt both.

There were years I wanted to escape you –
to believe that I was self-made.
Self-shaped.

Self-determined.

It is the folly of youth to think one can outrun oneself.
Still, it felt cleaner that way.
Simpler.

But inheritance is not a noose - it is a chain.

It is gravity that pulls whether you acknowledge it or not.

I have wrestled with your temper and your pride –
as I have my own.

With your fear of annihilation and your
instinct for dominance.

With your resilience...
the refusal to collapse when it would have been easier.

You taught me strength - but not how to temper it.
You taught me loyalty - but not how to judge it.
You taught me survival - but not how to stand down
when the danger had passed.

I stand before you not as judge, but as accomplice.
You navigated your own straits and carried fire across ages.

Now it burns in me –
stolen from the gods and given to a mortal.

My task is to tend it –
to decide what continues and what ends with me.

That is not betrayal.
It is evolution - with memory.

I honour your sacrifices and release you from your obligations.

I am neither your echo nor your rebellion.

I am the next integration.

TO MY PARENTS

You crossed oceans with little more than fear and hope.

The hope of a better life stronger
than the fear of the unknown.

That is a courage most people will never know.

Your minds were sharp,
but you worked where your bodies were needed.

You endured what I never had to and
gave me a stability you never knew.

For that, I honour you.
Not in words, but in deeds.

You kept Greece alive in our home,
speaking our language so we could learn it.

Even if it came at the expense of your own English.

You sent us to school when other children played.
To church, to parties, to dances filled with music,
joy and collective memory.

You made sure we knew where we came from.

That is the greatest inheritance you could give us.

I walked the path you cleared.

Factory floors.
Petrol pumps.
Courier vans.
Kitchen hand.

The work you knew all too well.
Long labour with little reward.

The work that built solid ground, not shifting sand.

But I did not stop there.

I saw a wider horizon and asked you to see it with me.

You chose not to.

Perhaps you were tired.
Perhaps you were content.
Perhaps you had already fought the battles
you were willing to fight.

I wanted expansion.
You wanted security.

Neither is wrong – only different.

I mistook your boundaries for mediocrity -
that was my own limitation, not yours.

Now I understand.

There were borders you would not cross –
and rooms too foreign to enter.

I entered boldly and you acknowledged it.

But that was not enough for me.
I wanted to see you move forward, too.

What began as distance became a divide.

I no longer wait for you to become what you are not.

You are my foundation.
I built beyond it - just as you hoped I would.

I will always speak the language you gave me.

And its music – especially Rebetika –
expresses something in me nothing else can.

Often to tears.

Always to dance.

TO MY BELOVED

There was a time when I believed strength meant
standing unyielding.

Winning the argument.
Holding ground.
Proving the point.

Ambition rewards that posture –
and the world often does, too.

Love does not.

Love exposes the cost of being right by teaching that victory
inside a union is defeat in disguise.

Every argument won at the expense of the bond
becomes a wound.

I had to learn that love cannot be adversarial...
a debate... a negotiation of territory.

Not a contest of who will claim the higher ground.

It is discipline.

To pause when pride pricks and anger seethes...
before words are spoken that cannot be taken back.

To protect the bond –
whatever the cost to ego and self-righteousness.

You never asked me to be smaller.
You required me to be steadier.

There is a difference.

Strength is easy when it confronts the world.
At home, it must be something else.

Ambition teaches us how to sharpen the blade.

Love teaches when not to draw it.

There were moments we both wanted to win –
after all, we are descended from warriors and Amazons.

In those moments, our love was overwhelmed –
almost shipwrecked.

Discretion was set aside for dominance -
and it was trust that was damaged.

Trust, once damaged, rarely returns unchanged.

Marriage is not the merging of two shadows.
It is the integration of two wills.

Not one overpowering the other.
Not one dissolving into the other.

Alignment and realignment -
a shared direction, set repeatedly.

The world speaks of passion as fire.

What endures is steadfastness.

The stubborn decision not to let
difference become distance.

And somewhere between endurance and despair,
Between pride and patience,
Between impulse and restraint -

I learned what devotion truly is.

Love is the storm.
The return is the vow.

TO MY SONS

There was a time when I believed fatherhood
meant protection.

Standing between you and the world like a colossus.

Anticipating every threat –
absorbing every blow before it reached you.

But I learned that protection is temporary –
preparation endures.

The world you enter is louder and
even more dangerous than the one I knew.

More distracted by nonsense.
More blinded by intolerance.
More eager to choose sides than to understand them.

You are prepared for the world - even this one.

What remains is the preparation of yourselves.

Strength will be expected of you –
success will be measured and performance tracked.

Character will not.

There will be pressure to mistake knowledge for wisdom.
To adopt outrage as identity.

To seek happiness in material things.

Do not become reactive in an age that rewards it.
Do not surrender your judgement to the crowd.

The task is not to win the argument –
but to keep your integrity intact.

Lies take the elevator.
The truth takes the stairs.

Gather the facts before you judge.
And when you judge, leave room for mercy –
you may one day depend on it.

A good man governs himself before he seeks
to influence others.

You were given more stability than I was.
More room to choose... more space to fail without collapsing.

That was deliberate.

Not so you could avoid hard work –
so, your effort could begin further forward.

The work ethic of your grandparents
built the ground beneath you.

The sacrifice of your parents lengthened the runway.

You inherit both.

But inheritance is not arrival... it is responsibility.

You will be tempted toward hubris.
Pride.
Flight without navigation.

Freedom is not recklessness -
and courage without discernment has undone many a man.

If I have succeeded in anything,
it was not in shaping you in my image –
but in giving you the space to outgrow
both image and shadow.

We gave you a longer runway.

You must still learn to fly –

Not toward the sun...
but toward your own horizon.

TO MY FRIENDS

There are men I laugh with.

And there are men I trust with my life – and my wife.

The difference is not enjoyment.

It is character.

Character is a man who tells you when you are wrong -
and still stands beside you once you know it.

A friend does not flatter in private then disappear in public.

He does not compete with your success or retreat
from your failure.

He corrects you... and then he stands.

A friend shares consequences.

If I am absent, you remain.
If I fall, you do not scatter.

Loyalty does not turn its back – convenience does.

True friendship is not convenient.

It demands sacrifice -
and an unwritten code, honoured.

My mother often repeated an old Greek saying:

Tell me who your friends are,
and I will tell you who you are.

It took me years to understand how true this was.

We are not only shaped by what we believe,
But by the company we keep.

TO MY ENEMIES

You were never the real conflict.

You were my test.

My teacher.

What angers a man can sharpen him.

Left unchecked, it hardens into hatred.
And hatred harms everyone.

I once believed retribution would bring me peace.

It deepened the wound –
and chained me to you long after the score was settled.

Peace began the day I stopped needing you to pay.

You did not defeat me.

You honed me.

And for that, I not only forgive you -
I also thank you.

Buddhist wisdom expresses this simply:

Your enemy is your greatest teacher.

It is a difficult lesson.

Those who oppose us most fiercely often reveal
what we have yet to master in ourselves.

TO MY YOUNGER SELF

You did not know where you belonged.

Too Greek for Australia - too Australian for Greece.

You wore your surname like a Scarlet Letter - and swallowed
insults before you had the language or courage to answer them.

You learned early that belonging was conditional -
so you tried to become strong enough not to care.

You retreated into books and imagined worlds.

The stories were universal –
but it was Olympus that felt like home.

They made you feel connected to something eternal –
that you were not alone.

Distance protected you -
but it also isolated you.

Eventually, you realised that being different
was not a weakness.

It was an advantage.

You learned the magic of the chameleon.
The raven.
The coyote –

shapeshifter, watcher, survivor.

To read a person before they read you.

To know if they were friend or foe.

The better you knew yourself,
the clearer others became.

You studied language.
Performance.
Masks.

English Literature and Drama were not accidents.
They were the formal education of instincts
you already possessed.

When you first read Shakespeare at fifteen,
you recognised something liberating.

All the world's a stage -
and you realised you could play it well.

But there is a cost to wearing masks well.
Masks provide power –
but power without purpose becomes consuming.

And the better you became at playing roles,
the harder it was to remember which one was yours.

Performance becomes competence.
Competence becomes reputation.

Reputation becomes expectation.

A prisoner of your own making.

The day you realised you no longer needed to prove you
belonged...you were free.

Confidence as a leader did not come from winning rooms,
it came from no longer needing to win them.

The masks did not disappear.
They became tools.

Somewhere in your mid-forties,
you finally settled into your own skin.

Sometimes it takes moments.
Sometimes decades.

You were never lost.

You were becoming.

Learning to embrace what you were born with –
your lineage, your talents, your karma.

Knowing what to keep - and what to let go.

Then adding to it.

Shaping yourself into your own image.

TO MY INNER COUNCIL

I did not think alone.

There are council members who dwell inside me.

They are not names displayed as intellectual ornaments.
They are interior companions - dwelling in heart and mind.

They do not introduce themselves. They reveal themselves -
when I need them, and in the pages that follow.

A blind poet who suggests progress over perfection.
A questioning Athenian when conclusions
come too quickly.
An Olympian who cautions against
impulse without strategy.
A wanderer who understands the cost of
not returning home.
A dissident who warns against comfort becoming compromise
and mediocrity.
A monk who insists that kindness
is man's most potent weapon.
A beloved who reminds me of what matters now.
They do not speak in sentences.

They surface as tension - and they rarely agree.

That is the point.

Wisdom is not the possession of a single voice.

It is the instinct to know which voice to follow in each
moment - including your own.

This I have learned:

When I admire their work, I keep it alive.

When I allow them to dwell within me, I keep them alive.

Their influence is an imprint on my DNA –
like karma, carried and transformed across lifetimes.

THE GROUND BETWEEN

"The virtue of a man lies in the mean between excess and deficiency." – Aristotle.

We have mistaken individuality for separateness -
and the consequence is fragmentation.

This is now the central problem of our time.

Not conflict.
Not disagreement.

Fragmentation.

What began as a recognition of uniqueness has calcified into
isolation – an inner state that sets us at odds with ourselves...
and then with the world.

We are complex creatures who have built
complex systems and societies.

To survive that complexity, we created distinctions –
concepts that simplified reality and
created shared understanding.

Self or other.
Friend or foe.
Left or right.
Heaven or hell.

These distinctions are useful –
they describe; they clarify.

But somewhere along the way,
we began to believe we must choose between them.

Duality is not the enemy.
Division is.

We were meant to embrace opposites –
not inhabit them exclusively.

The fracture appears small.
It hides in a single word:

OR.

Are you left, or right?
Logical, or emotional?
Religious, or agnostic?

OR simplifies... but it also divides.

I am this or that.
I belong here - not there.

Much of the conflict we face arises from –
and is amplified by – this error.

Much of it would soften under one corrective word:

AND.

The word is simple.
The discipline – difficult.

There was a time I believed clarity required decisiveness.

Choose a side.
Take a position.
Defend it.

It seemed to work –
at least on the surface.

In meetings, I was quick.
Articulate.
Certain.

I was often right.

But over time, something became clear.

The room would go quiet...
But not aligned.

People would agree...
But not commit.

And outcomes would stall –
not because the answer was wrong,
but because the process had excluded them.

And sometimes, the cost was not just delay.

It was trust.

There were moments where people stopped bringing their full thinking into the room.

Not because they did not have it –
but because they did not believe they would be heard.

And that is the intangible cost of drawing conclusions too quickly.

You do not just lose perspective –
You lose participation.

It took longer than it should have for me to realise:

Being right is not the same as being effective.

Leadership is not the act of deciding.

It is the discipline of holding multiple perspectives long enough for the right decision to emerge.

Because integration is not intellectual.

It is psychological.

It requires something we are rarely taught:

To hold tension... without collapsing into certainty.

To resist the instinct to choose sides when complexity
demands understanding.

To remain present in contradiction...
without immediate resolution.

A person sits at the dinner table.
Across from them, someone expresses a view they
disagree with.

They feel it immediately – the tightening in the chest...
the sharpening of thought... the impulse to respond.

To defend.
To correct.
To win.

In that moment, there are two paths.

One leads to reaction.
The other to restraint.

If they react, the conversation escalates.

Positions harden.
Voices rise.
Neither side listens.

Both leave more certain – and more divided.

But if they restrain themselves... even briefly...
something else becomes possible.

Curiosity.
Understanding.
A question instead of a rebuttal.
Connection instead of escalation.

This is the ground between.
And most of us never learn how to stand there.

A mother argues with her daughter.
A husband with his wife.
A friend with a friend.

In each moment, the same pattern emerges.

The need to be right...
overtakes the responsibility to remain connected.

Victory becomes more important than the bond.
And so, the bond weakens.
Not in a single moment –
but across many small fractures.

Until one day, distance replaces closeness.
And both wonder how it happened.

I have sat in that silence.
Felt the distance I helped create.

Realised – too late in the moment –
that what I protected was my position.
And what I damaged was the relationship.

And no argument, however righteous at the time,
is worth that trade.

Being wrong is not the danger.
It is being blind to what standing your ground costs.

At scale, the same pattern repeats.

Communities fracture into tribes.
Tribes into factions.
Factions into enemies.

Each convinced of its own correctness.
Each blind to its own incompleteness.

Social media accelerates this.
It rewards certainty.
Amplifies outrage.
Punishes nuance.

And so, people form their positions instead of
examining them.

Identity replaces enquiry.
Belonging replaces truth.
And fragmentation becomes culture.

The work of integration is standing between opposing forces -
without being consumed by either.

Odysseus between Scylla and Charybdis -
the monster and the whirlpool.

Too far one way – destruction.
Too far the other – destruction.

The path is narrow.
And it requires awareness... restraint... judgement.

It requires discipline.

Consider the athlete.
Too much intensity and the body breaks.
Too little and it never adapts.
Potential exists in tension.
Not in extremes.

Consider the mind.
Too much certainty - and it closes.
Too much doubt – and it collapses.
Wisdom exists in balance, not in absolutes.

Consider freedom.
Without responsibility, it becomes chaos.
Consider responsibility.
Without freedom, it becomes oppression.

Each requires the other.
Neither survives alone.

Integration does not begin in institutions,
it begins in the interior life.

But to understand how it is possible...
we must examine something more fundamental.

The relationship between cause – and choice.

I had a challenging conversation with a young man
who argued - very convincingly - that everything is determined.

By our biology.
Our upbringing.
Our environment.

And to a point, he is right.

We do not choose our genes.
Our parents.
The conditions that shape us.

Even our impulses arise before we are aware of them.

Thought appears.
Emotion follows.

That is the chain of causality.

But it is not the full picture.

Because something else happens next.

Awareness.

And with it... a pause.

Between what we feel...
and what we do.

In that space, something becomes possible.

Not control in the absolute sense.

But influence.

Not freedom from cause...
but freedom within it.

To acknowledge the emotion.
To accept it.
To embrace it.
To integrate it.

And to choose how we respond.

If that space did not exist...
there would be no restraint.

No responsibility.
No morality.

Only reaction.

And that is why O'Malley's Bar by Nick Cave
is so confronting.

A man walks into a bar...
and kills everyone inside.

Cold.
Methodical.
Total.

And the uncomfortable question sits underneath it.

If he had no choice...
if he was only a product of his causes...
then how can he be held responsible?

But that question exposes the flaw.

Because even in the darkest extremes...
the question remains the same.

To act – or not to act.

And that is where the argument either holds –
or collapses.

But restraint exists.

Which means we are not identical to our impulses.

We are shaped by them...
but not completely bound by them.

And that is where integration lives.

Before nations polarise, individuals do.
Before systems fail, minds do.

I have seen this play out at scale.

Teams divided not by capability...
But by perspective.

Functions protecting territory instead of solving problems.

Meetings where positions were defended long after they
stopped making sense.

Not because people were incapable -
Because they identified with only their position.

To change their view felt like losing.

So, they stood their ground - and progress slowed.

What was needed was not more intelligence.

It was integration.

The ability to step back from the position...
And return to the problem.

The world that we inhabit is the amplified expression of
tensions we refuse to reconcile within ourselves –
or do not yet recognise.

It took me years to recognise this in myself.

To see how quickly I moved toward certainty.

How easily I categorised.
Judged.
Agreed or disagreed.
Right or wrong.

With me or against me.

It felt efficient.
It felt strong.

But it was incomplete.

Because every time I simplified too quickly,
I lost something.

Context.
Nuance.
Understanding.

And often – the person in front of me.

A man who cannot hold two opposing truths within himself
will demand that the world resolves them for him.

Usually by force.
Or ideology.
Or at the expense of others.

This is how fragmentation scales.

From discomfort...
To division...
To conflict...
To destruction.

History is not short of examples.

Empires fall.
Societies fracture.

Not because disagreement exists –
because integration fails.

And when it fails at scale,
something more dangerous emerges.

Not just disagreement... but dehumanisation.

The other side is no longer wrong.
They are no longer misguided.
They are no longer even human.

And once that line is crossed, history becomes predictable.

Because what we refuse to integrate...
We eventually seek to eliminate.

The cost is not abstract.
It is personal.
It is relational.
It is civilisational.

Families break where understanding could have
held them together.

Friendships dissolve where patience could have
preserved them.

Communities fracture where dialogue could have
sustained them.

Institutions collapse where balance could have
stabilised them.

And yet the solution remains the same.

It is not found first in systems.
It is found in individuals.
In moments.

In decisions so small they often go unnoticed.

To pause instead of reacting.
To listen instead of asserting.
To question instead of concluding.
To hold both... instead of choosing one.

The real divide is not between us.
It is within us.

And until we learn to reconcile it there...
We will continue to fight it everywhere else.

The first tension we encounter is not ideological.

It is human.

Fear and hope.

Fear contracts.
Hope projects.

Both are necessary –
but both create imbalance when left unchecked.

And so, the work begins there.

FEAR AND HOPE

Fear is a fundamental instinct.

It protects us from danger.
It sharpens attention.

It reminds us that the world contains risks
that must be respected.

Without fear, human beings would not survive long.

Hope is equally fundamental.

It allows us to imagine futures that do not yet exist.
It gives meaning to struggle.
It makes endurance possible.

Without hope, survival would lose its purpose.

Every human life unfolds between these two forces.

Fear pulls us toward caution.
Hope pulls us toward possibility.

Both are necessary – but can mislead.

Unchecked, fear constricts growth.
Unanchored, hope becomes dissatisfaction.

Being tossed between them is exhausting.

Energy depletes.
Rest becomes difficult.

We try to eliminate what unsettles us instead of
restoring proportion.

Ecosystems are not healed by eradication.
They are restored by realignment.

When the inner world tilts, the outer world mirrors it.
When enough individuals tilt, the tribe tilts.

Communities are not merely groups of individuals.
They are shared emotional climates.

Fear clusters.
Hope clusters.

We gather with those who mirror what we carry.

The anxious seek protection.
The disillusioned seek restoration.
The idealistic seek transformation.

The tribe feels stabilising – an anchor in rough seas.

If built on unexamined fear, it becomes aggressive.
If built on unexamined hope, it becomes defensive.

In both cases, imbalance multiplies.

Aesop told a simple story.

A traveller walking through a forest heard a branch snap
behind him.
Fear told him a wolf was stalking him.
Hope told him it was only the wind.
When he turned, it was a deer.

Fear sharpened his sense.
Hope kept him from running blindly.

Wisdom required both.

Technology has made this visible at scale.

Social media has become the nervous system of the tribe.

It does not create fear – it accelerates it.
It does not invent outrage – it amplifies it.
Reaction replaces reflection.

Like truth and lies, outrage travels faster than verification.
Positions calcify.

Tribes fortify, preparing for war.

When tribes tilt long enough, institutions tilt with them.

Policies become reactive.
Leadership becomes performative.
Discourse becomes combative.

Nations are ecosystems, too.

When enough individuals and institutions are knocked off
their axis, the nation is impacted.

We call it instability.
Polarisation.
Crisis.

But beneath the headlines, it is the same mechanism.

Imbalance multiplied.

The world feels unstable.
But the world is a reflection.

The question is not whether it is off its axis.

The question is:

Are you?
Are we?

REASON AND INTUITION

There are things the body knows before the mind
has formed a question.

The hairs that rise.
The chest that tightens.
The breath that shallows -
before you understand why.

We call it instinct.
Intuition.
Spidey-sense.

Whatever the name - it is older than language.
Older than reason.
And far more honest.

I have felt it many times –
twice in a way that changed me.

Standing on a mountain in pitch black, watching something
move across the sky in a pattern no satellite follows –
circling, zigging, unhurried, deliberate.

My reason said: satellite.
My body said: something else.

Thirty-five years later, I still see it.
The hairs still rise.
The heart still races.

The second time, I was on a back porch, mid-thought,
mid-cigarette - thinking about the gods, of all things.

It appeared again.
Different path.
Same unmistakable movement.

Same response in the body.

This time, instead of reaching for an explanation,
I opened myself to the question.

I cannot explain what I saw.
But I can feel that it matters.

That is the difference between reason and intuition.

Reason demands an answer.
Intuition is comfortable with mystery.

We live in an age that worships reason.
And reason has served us well.

It built the cities.
Mapped the genome.
Sent machines beyond the edge of the solar system.

But somewhere along the way, we made a mistake.

We began to treat intuition as the enemy of reason.
Primitive. Unreliable. Embarrassing.

Something to be explained away –
or medicated into silence.

And in doing so, we lost something essential.

Because reason and intuition are not rivals.

They are partners.

Two ways of knowing the same reality.

Reason examines the structure of the world.
Intuition feels its weight.

One asks: how does this work?
The other asks: does this feel right?

Both questions matter.
Neither is sufficient alone.

A civilisation that has lost touch with its intuition has lost
touch with its conscience.

And conscience, it turns out, is not a product of logic.
It is a product of feeling.

The child knows this instinctively.

Before language.
Before argument.
Before the sophisticated architecture of justification
is constructed -

the child feels the wrongness of cruelty.
Flinches at suffering.
Reaches toward the wounded.

We are born with the signal intact.

Then we are educated out of it.

Nietzsche understood the danger.

A clever man, he observed, can justify anything.

And that is precisely what we have become.

Clever.

Clever enough to construct airtight arguments for
looking away.
Clever enough to find legal frameworks for illegal acts.
Clever enough to call the bombing of children a matter
of complexity.

There is a word for what happens when an educated,
civilised people construct sophisticated justifications for the
destruction of another.

We know that word.

We learned it in the middle of the last century.

When the most educated nation in Europe -
a nation of philosophers, composers, scientists -
reasoned itself into genocide.

Bureaucrats signed the forms.
Lawyers wrote the briefs.
Intellectuals provided the frameworks.

And the intuition of millions screamed -
and was silenced by the most dangerous weapon ever deployed
against human conscience.

Sophisticated argument.

We said: never again.

And we meant it.

Until we didn't.

Because our intuition is not confused about history repeating.
It never was.

The body knows.
The chest tightens.
The breath shallows.

The child under the rubble today
is the same child as last century.

The mother is the same mother,
and her face needs no translation.

That is the signal.

But reason - deployed not in search of truth, but in defence of
position - has learned to override it.

To flood the signal with noise.
To replace the feeling with a framework.
To turn conscience into a debate.

And so, we scroll past the rubble.
Past the small shoes.
Past the faces of mothers.

Not because we do not feel it.

But because we have been given permission not to act on
what we feel.

That permission is called sophistication.

It is, in fact, a kind of death.

As my son observed -
we do not scroll past because we do not care.

We scroll past because the world now has too many windows.

And suffering, seen through enough of them, becomes noise.

The instinct is to look outward -
at what is vast and distant and beyond our reach.

Rather than inward - at what is close enough to change.

When we are consumed by the problems we cannot solve -
there is no room left for the ones we can.

And as my wife observed - with age comes another layer.

We have seen it before.

The same wars.
The same faces.
The same arguments dressed in new clothes.

And we learn - not from cruelty, but from exhaustion -
to look away.

That is not apathy.

It is the cost of having paid attention for too long.

I write this as the grandson of people who fled persecution.

Who know what it is to be the ones the world reasoned itself
into ignoring.

My intuition does not get to choose who deserves its signal.

Neither does yours.

It is a human one.

The most dangerous person in any room is not the one who
feels too much.

It is the one who has reasoned themselves out of feeling
anything at all.

History does not remember them as sophisticated.
It remembers them as complicit.

I am not arguing against reason.

I am arguing for integration.

Reason without intuition produces capability
without conscience.

Intuition without reason produces passion without direction.

But when they work together -
when the goosebumps and the argument arrive
at the same conclusion -
you are close to something true.

Something that cannot be justified away.

On a mountain, in the dark, watching something move across
the sky - I did not need a framework.

I needed to be present enough to feel it.

A silent whisper.

A hint of perfume.

Of intoxication.

That is what we are at risk of losing.

Not our intelligence.

Our capacity to be moved into action.

POWER AND RESTRAINT

"He who cannot command himself must obey." –
Friedrich Nietzsche.

Power appears in many forms.

The power over oneself:
self-mastery.

The power over others: leadership –
sometimes bestowed, sometimes imposed.

And the power over nature.

This is the power civilisation celebrates most.

The power that builds cities... technologies... comforts that
would have seemed miraculous to our ancestors.

It is also the power with the greatest potential for harm,
if corrupted.

When a species learns it can bend the world to its will, it begins
to believe it is above the laws that govern it.

Above the laws that sustain life in balance.

This is the hubris of humanity.

The laws of nature are not suggestions.

They are conditions.

A man who believes he is above the law is dangerous.

A civilisation that believes it is above the laws of nature
becomes toxic.

Power without restraint eventually destroys the very world that
made it possible.

The most profound form of power is not domination –
it is discipline.

The discipline to harness strength -
and direct it toward constructive purpose.

Strength with restraint.
Power with temperance.
Purpose with responsibility.

ANGER AND FORGIVENESS

"Sing, O goddess, the anger of Achilles..." – Homer.

Anger remembers.
Forgiveness decides whether the past continues.

Few forces shape human relationships more powerfully
than anger.

It fractures families.
Divides communities.
Turns brothers into enemies.

Yet anger is not inherently destructive.

At times, anger has been the force that has exposed injustice –
and demanded change.

Without anger, many of the freedoms people now consider
fundamental would never have emerged.

Democracy.
Fair labour.
Civil rights.

Directed toward injustice,
anger can become a catalyst for reform.

But anger untethered from wisdom becomes
something else entirely.

It corrodes judgement.
Narrows perspective.
Perpetuates the very harm it claims to resist.

Forgiveness is not the denial of harm.
Nor is it the absolution.

It is a decision - that the past will not dictate the future.

Forgiveness must begin with forgiving ourselves.

Human beings carry regret.
Shame.
Memory.

Mistakes are inevitable.

Without the capacity to forgive ourselves,
the past becomes a prison.

The next place forgiveness must radiate to is those closest to us.

Parents.
Family.
Those who shaped our early lives.

Every generation passes forward both wisdom and wounds.
To mature is to embrace both.

And eventually forgiveness must extend even further, towards
those who have caused us genuine harm.

That is the most difficult form of forgiveness.

But without it, resentment becomes
a permanent companion.

Homer tells of Achilles.

When Patroclus fell,
his anger burned so fiercely it reshaped the war.

Yet even he returned Hector's body to his grieving father.

In that moment, anger yielded to something deeper.
Even the fiercest anger must one day yield to mercy.

Anger, like fear and hope, is part of the human condition.
It cannot be eliminated - nor should it be.

Anger is often the forge from which societies build justice.
But untethered, it becomes destructive.

Ill-directed, it rarely travels alone.
It rides with ignorance and hate.

Anger may ignite change.
Forgiveness allows healing when the struggle is over.

Without it, conflict becomes perpetual.
With it, renewal becomes possible.

The task is not to eliminate anger.

It is to direct it wisely –
and to recognise when the time has come for forgiveness to do
the work that anger cannot.

COMMUNICATION AND CONNECTION

Modern civilisation has mastered communication –
but forgotten connection.

We are now more informed than ever,
yet increasingly lonely.

Never has it been easier to transmit information.

Messages travel across continents in seconds.
Images and opinions circle the globe in real time.
Every individual now carries a device capable of
reaching millions.

The technical achievement is extraordinary.

Yet something essential has been lost.

Conversation.

Human beings evolved in small communities where
communication carried weight.

Words were spoken face to face.
Tone mattered.
Gesture mattered.
Silence mattered.

Disagreement required courage –
because the other person was present.

Modern communication has removed much of that friction.

We can broadcast opinions without looking into the eyes of
those who hear them.

We can argue without consequence.
Condemn without reflection.
Perform outrage without restraint.

What is lost is connection.

Connection requires more than the exchange of information.

It requires attention.
Patience.
The willingness to understand another perspective
before rejecting it.

These qualities develop slowly.

Modern communication rewards speed.

Instant reactions.
Instant judgements.
Instant tribes.

The result is a paradox.

We are surrounded by voices - but starved of conversation.
People speak constantly - but listen rarely.

Noise increases - while understanding diminishes.

Technology did not invent this.

Human beings have always gravitated toward those who
confirm their beliefs.

Modern platforms accelerate it.

Algorithms learn what we prefer –
and deliver more of it.

Disagreement becomes unfamiliar.
Nuance becomes inconvenient.

Online communities slowly become echo chambers.

When communication fragments, societies begin to lose the
ability to deliberate.

Discourse becomes performance.
Positions harden.
Cooperation becomes difficult.

The danger is not disagreement.
Healthy societies require disagreement.
The danger is the disappearance of conversation.

Without conversation, there is no understanding.
Without understanding there is no trust.

My mother used to repeat an old Greek saying:

Only by being kind can you change someone's mind.

It sounds almost naive in a world that rewards
aggression and outrage.

But it contains a psychological truth modern society
has forgotten.

Kindness and empathy are the most powerful
agents of influence.

FREEDOM AND RESPONSIBILITY

Freedom is one of the most powerful ideas
a civilisation can summon.

It has launched revolutions, toppled tyrants and inspired
people to risk everything to live without subjugation.

Something has changed in the way we understand it.

What was once a civic right is increasingly treated
as a personal entitlement.

Freedom has been separated from the obligations
that sustain it.

This misunderstanding becomes most visible in the first
institution – the family.

Freedom does not mean abandoning responsibility for those
dependent on you –
yet this confusion has become common.

Many people now place their personal freedom above the
stability of the family itself.

Springsteen wrote a song about a man who went out for a ride
and never went back.

He called it a hungry heart.

The Buddhists recognised the same thing -
just with a different face.

When difficulty arises in a relationship, it is often taken as
evidence that something better exists elsewhere.

The greener grass.

But it is only greener from a distance.

Up close it requires the same work.
The same patience.
The same compromise.
The same sacrifice.

When people run from one relationship to another seeking
greater happiness, they do not escape the real source of the
problem – it travels with them.

Baggage that cannot be left behind.

Difficulty is not a defect in relationships.

It is a feature.

Human beings are imperfect.
Living closely exposes it.

Freedom within a family does not mean
escape from responsibility.

It means the courage and discipline to face problems -
and grow through them.

The culture surrounding us reinforces
the opposite message.

We live in a civilisation built on consumer logic.
Replace rather than repair.

What was once built to last is now built to be replaced.

That logic has spread beyond goods into relationships.

When difficulties arise – and they will –
many replace rather than repair.

People are not appliances.
Relationships should not be disposable.

When the habit of replacement becomes cultural, the
institutions that sustain a civilisation begin to weaken.

Families fracture.
Communities destabilise.

Freedom becomes confused with the absence of obligation.

Responsibility begins to feel like oppression.

A society of free people cannot survive if freedom is mistaken
for doing whatever one wishes.

That does not produce liberty.
It produces disorder.

The ancient Greeks understood something that modern
societies often forget.

Freedom begins with self-governance.

As Aristotle observed – and Nietzsche later echoed –

A man who cannot govern himself must eventually be
governed by others.

Responsibility is the foundation of liberty.

It is the unspoken agreement that allows millions of strangers
to share a society without devouring one another.

Without self-governance, freedom becomes indistinguishable
from selfishness and entitlement.

Multiplied across millions,
this produces a dysfunctional society.

History is full of examples.

But it rarely records the moment a society begins to fail -
because it almost never happens all at once.

Freedom is rarely lost in a single act.

It is surrendered gradually... often by those who misunderstand what it requires.

The greatest threat to freedom is not tyranny.
It is immaturity.

A civilisation cannot be more responsible than the people who compose it.

Which returns us to where it begins – the individual.

Freedom and responsibility are not competing principles.
They are symbiotic.

Responsibility produces restraint.
Restraint protects freedom.

SYSTEMS THAT DEVOUR AND
SYSTEMS THAT SERVE

Institutions are created to serve society.

When power and gain distort their purpose, they begin to devour the people they were meant to protect.

Marcus Aurelius said that:

"What injures the hive injures the bee."

But that is only half the story.

What injures the hive injures the bee.
And what injures the bee injures the hive.

Every civilisation depends on institutions.

Governments.
Courts.
Churches.
Schools.

These systems organise cooperation at a scale that individuals cannot sustain alone.

At their best, institutions stabilise society.

They protect rights.
Coordinate effort.

Preserve knowledge.

Institutions do not remain healthy without cultivation –
and sometimes that requires controlled burning.

Like individuals, they are vulnerable to
dysfunction and obsolescence.

Power accumulates.
Intentions waver.

Gradually, systems designed to serve society begin
to serve themselves.

History offers many examples.

Empires that began as guardians of order
became instruments of extraction.

Governments built to protect citizens have become
bureaucracies that protect their own authority.

Markets designed to generate prosperity became mechanisms
for concentrating wealth and influence.

The transformation happens slowly... almost imperceptibly.

Rules expand and encroach.
Power centralises.
Accountability erodes.

The institution that once served society

begins to consume it.

Much of this distortion happens from a deeper feature of
human nature.

Human beings rarely remain satisfied with sufficiency.

We pursue more.

More wealth.
More influence.
More security.
More control.

Buddhism offers a striking metaphor.

The Hungry Ghost.

A being with enormous appetite –
and a throat too narrow to satisfy it.

No matter how much it consumes, it remains starving.

This is the nature of unchecked appetite.

A Buddhist teacher once described desire to his students.

He held up a cup of tea and asked them what would happen if
it were filled beyond its edge.
The tea would spill and be wasted.

So, it is with human appetite.

Enough sustains life.
Too much begins to consume it.

When individuals driven by this hunger gain influence within
institutions, carnage follows.

The system begins to reflect the appetites of those
who control it.

Policies shift towards accumulation.
Decisions prioritise preservation of power.

Institutions transform from guardians to predators.

This pattern appears across political,
economic and cultural systems.

The ideology may differ - the mechanism is the same.

Systems that lose connection to the people they were created to
serve eventually begin to devour them.

Which is why healthy civilisations must continually review and
reset the balance between institutional power and
civic purpose.

Institutions must remain accountable to the societies that
created them.

And citizens within those societies must remain vigilant.

Institutions do not corrupt on their own.

They reflect the values, appetites and maturity of the people who run them.

When individuals pursue power without restraint, the systems they build mirror that imbalance.

When institutions remain anchored in responsibility and service, they sustain societies for generations.

The question every civilisation must confront is simple:

Are its institutions serving the people?
Or feeding upon them?

LEGACY AND CONTINUITY

"People are trapped in history and history is trapped in them."
– James Baldwin.

Every civilisation lives within a longer current of time.

Individuals are temporary.
Generations pass.

But ideas, values and institutions travel forward.

Legacy is the mechanism through which this
transmission occurs.

Some of what we inherit is material.

Cities.
Technology.
Art.
Scientific knowledge accumulated over centuries.

But much of what we inherit is intangible.

Stories.
Customs.
Beliefs about what is right and wrong.
Assumptions about how society should function.

These are passed from one generation to the next.

Parents to children.
Teachers to students.
Communities to those who grow up within them.

Every generation therefore receives two inheritances.

Wisdom.
And error.

What we inherit is not only knowledge - but the wisdom with which previous generations used it.

Or failed to.

Because knowledge alone does not guarantee maturity.

A society becomes technologically advanced while remaining morally confused.

Which brings us to the question of legacy.

What survives us is not merely what we build.

It is what we transmit.

The values we pass on.
The habits we normalise.
The wisdom – or ignorance – we carry forward.

Every generation shapes the inheritance of the next.

Sometimes intentionally.

Sometimes unconsciously.

Children absorb far more than what adults claim
to teach them.

They absorb how power is exercised.
How conflict is handled.
How responsibility is embraced - or avoided.

They inherit not only knowledge, but character.

And over time, these imprints accumulate.

A civilisation therefore becomes the expression of the values
repeated across generations.

When those values emphasise responsibility, discipline and
cooperation, societies tend to thrive.

When they reward selfishness, excess and short-term gain,
the result is dysfunction.

Legacy is not remembrance.
It is continuity.

The transmission of patterns that shape the future long after
the individuals are gone.

The question each generation must eventually confront
is simple.

What are we passing forward?

And what will remain of us when we are no longer here?

One thing is certain:

The true measure of legacy is not wealth left behind –
but lives left richer.

KNOWLEDGE AND WISDOM

Human civilisation has never possessed more knowledge
than it does today.

Libraries once accessible only to scholars now fit inside a device
that rests in a pocket.

Scientific discovery continues to accelerate -
and we can all now keep pace with its findings.

Information travels instantly across continents, accumulating
at a scale previous generations could not have imagined.

In many ways, humanity has never been more informed.

Yet something essential remains scarce.

Wisdom.

Knowledge tells us how things work.
Wisdom asks how they should be used.

Knowledge builds powerful tools.
Wisdom determines whether those tools serve humanity -
or harm it.

When knowledge grows faster than wisdom, imbalance
becomes dangerous.

Information overloads.

Judgement weakens.

Societies become increasingly capable of solving technical problems – while struggling to resolve human ones.

The problem is not knowledge itself.

Knowledge is indispensable.

Scientific discovery has transformed human life in extraordinary ways.

Medicine has extended lifespans.
Engineering has reshaped cities.
Technology has connected the world.

But knowledge without wisdom lacks direction.

It produces capability without discernment.

And capability without discernment is one of the greatest risks to a civilisation.

Wisdom requires something knowledge alone cannot provide.

Experience.
Reflection.
Humility.
The recognition of limits.

Wisdom is earned slowly.

It develops through failure, responsibility and the observation of consequences over time.

That is why civilisations have traditionally placed such value on elders, philosophers and teachers.

Not because they possessed more information - but because they possessed greater perspective.

Modern culture often inverts this.

We celebrate novelty.
Reward speed.
Elevate those who accumulate influence quickly –
even when their judgement remains untested.

The result is a paradox.

The people capable of creating powerful tools are not always best equipped to judge whether they should exist.

Knowledge created the tools.

Wisdom arrived later –
often after the consequences become visible.

Which brings us to the most important question:

Who should lead a civilisation that possesses immense knowledge and power –
but uncertain wisdom and restraint?

Leadership requires more than intelligence.
It requires discernment.

The ability to recognise which knowledge matters,
which voice deserves trust -
and which paths lead to long-term prosperity rather than short-
term advantage.

A society that entrusts power to those who possess knowledge
but lack wisdom becomes unstable.

A society that values wisdom but rejects knowledge
becomes stagnant.

The health of a civilisation therefore depends on the
integration of both.

We need knowledge.
The wisdom to use it well -
and the discernment to entrust power only to those who
possess both.

But knowledge and wisdom, for all their power,
can only take us so far.

At the edge of what we know...
something else begins.

SCIENCE AND SPIRITUALITY

For centuries, science and spirituality have been
presented as enemies.

One deals in proof.

The other in faith.

One measures what is visible.
The other senses what is not.

But this conflict is a misunderstanding -
and a costly one.

They are not rivals.

They are two different instruments listening for
the same signal.

Science advances by lifting the veil -
measuring, mapping, proving what was once mystery.

But the veil never disappears.

Every answer reveals a deeper question.
The further science reaches, the vaster the unknown becomes.

That is not a failure of science.

It is its most honest finding.

And it is precisely where spirituality begins.

Einstein understood this.

He did not speak of God in the conventional sense.
He spoke of mystery.

Of the cosmic religious feeling - the sense of awe before a
universe too vast and ordered to be accidental.

He believed that the most beautiful emotion a human being
could experience was the sense of the mysterious.

That it was the source of all true science.

And all true art.

Einstein stood at the veil and felt what was behind it -
not with instruments, but with wonder.

The Buddha stood at the same veil.

But he approached it differently.

He did not theorise about the universe.
He turned inward - and observed the mind with the same
rigour a scientist applies to the physical world.

Sit. Watch. See for yourself.

No doctrine.

No faith required.
Only attention.

What he found was not a god.
Not a reward.
Not a set of rules.

He found that beneath the noise of thought, beneath the
weight of ego, fear and desire - something else exists.

Something quiet.
Something vast.
Something that feels, unmistakably, like connection.

Science is beginning to sense it too.

In the early twentieth century, physicists made a discovery so
strange it unsettled even those who made it.

Two particles, once connected, remain connected -
across any distance.

Instantaneously.

Without any visible mechanism.

Einstein called it spooky action at a distance.

He was deeply troubled by it.

Because it suggested something that reason alone could not
accommodate.

That separateness - the fundamental assumption of the
physical world - may be, at some level, an illusion.

Which is precisely what the Buddha had said.

Twenty-five centuries earlier.

Without a laboratory.
Without instruments.

Through nothing but sustained, disciplined attention to the
nature of reality.

The scientist and the mystic did not set out to find
the same thing.

They were not even asking the same question.

And yet - at the edges of what each could reach - they arrived at
the same border.

The same veil.
The same trembling sense that what lies behind it is
not emptiness.
Not randomness.
Not indifference.
But something that connects.
Something that holds.

Every contemplative tradition that has gone deep enough has
returned with the same report.

The Sufi and the Yogi.
The Christian saint in prayer.
The Buddhist master in stillness.
The Philosopher in the cave.

They did not all speak the same language.
They did not share the same doctrine.
But they described the same experience.

Beneath the separateness - there is unity.
Beneath the fear - there is peace.
Beneath the noise - there is silence.

And in that silence -
there is something that can only be described as love.

Not romantic love.

Not the love that rises and falls with circumstance.

Something older.

Something that does not require a reason - or a recipient.

A love that is not an emotion but a condition.

The ground of everything.

The Buddhists call it compassion -
but in its deepest form it is not pity for suffering.

It is the recognition that all suffering arises from
the same source.

Separation.

The illusion that we are alone.

That we are distinct.

That what happens to another does not happen to us.

Science calls the opposite of this entanglement.

Spirituality calls it grace.

Every tradition calls it something different.

But behind every name - the same veil.
And behind the veil - the same light.

THE GROUND OF EVERYTHING

I did not know what I was writing when I began.

I thought I was writing about tension.

About the space between opposing forces -
and how to navigate it without being consumed.

That is what I set out to explore.

But somewhere between Knowledge and Wisdom...
something shifted.
Hairs pricked.
Senses tingled.

I began to see that the tensions were not the subject.

They were the surface.

Beneath every opposition - fear and hope, reason and intuition,
power and restraint - something else was present.

The same ground.

The same source.

What the mystics found in stillness.
What the physicists found at the edges of matter.
What every human being touches in their deepest moments of
love, grief, or wonder.

We do not live between opposites.

We live within a wholeness that appears to us as opposites –
because we are not yet still enough to see the unity.

Each of us contains the ground of everything.

So, the work, as always, begins with us -
slowly, with kindness and awareness...
the discipline of integration.

NOTES

The following sources informed or inspired passages in this
book. They are offered for those who wish to go deeper.
In order of appearance:

Aristotle - The Nicomachean Ethics.
The foundational text of Western moral philosophy, written in the
fourth century BC. He understood integration before the word existed.

Shakespeare - All the world's a stage, As You Like It.
The line that gave a young Greek-Australian boy the sword and the
shield he needed to navigate a dangerous world.

Buddhist wisdom - Your enemy is your greatest teacher.
A central teaching of Tibetan Buddhism, attributed to various masters
across centuries. The hardest lessons are the most useful ones.

Homer - The Odyssey.
The oldest story of a man trying to find his way home through forces
that want to consume him. He navigated the narrowest paths, Hades
itself and god-sent storms to honour his vow.

Nick Cave - O'Malley's Bar, from Murder Ballads, 1996.
A confronting meditation on free will and moral responsibility. If we
are only products of our causes, how can we be held accountable?
A question with no answer?

Aesop - Fables, sixth century BC.
The oldest wisdom tradition in the Western world, passed down orally
before it was ever written. A traveller in a forest. Fear, hope, and a
deer. The simplest stories contain the deepest truths.

*Friedrich Nietzsche - Thus Spoke Zarathustra and
Beyond Good and Evil.
The most misunderstood philosopher of the modern era.
Nietzsche did not celebrate power - he demanded that power be earned
through self-mastery. He who cannot command himself must obey.
A dissident who warned against comfort becoming compromise.*

*Homer - The Iliad.
The oldest story of rage and its consequences. Achilles, the greatest
warrior who ever lived, undone not by an enemy but by his own anger.
Yet even he found mercy. The Iliad is not a war story. It is a story about
what war costs the human soul.*

*Bruce Springsteen - Hungry Heart, from The River, 1980.
A song about a man who went out for a ride and never went back.
Springsteen understood what the Buddhists had known for centuries –
that unchecked appetite devours everything it was meant to protect.
Including love.*

*Aristotle - Politics.
A man who cannot govern himself must eventually be governed by
others. The foundation of every functioning democracy ever built.
Two thousand years later, we are still learning this.*

*Marcus Aurelius - Meditations.
The private journal of a Roman Emperor who never intended it to be
read. The most honest book ever written by someone in power.
What injures the hive injures the bee.
He understood that leadership is inseparable from service.*

*Buddhist cosmology - The Hungry Ghost.
A being with an enormous appetite and a throat too narrow to satisfy
it. The most precise metaphor ever conceived for unchecked human
desire. It appears in institutions, in markets, in politics -
and in each of us, if we are not paying attention.*

James Baldwin - Notes of a Native Son and collected essays.
The most honest American writer of the twentieth century.
People are trapped in history and history is trapped in them.
Baldwin understood that the past is never past -
it lives in the body, in the culture, in the silence between generations.

Albert Einstein - Ideas and Opinions and various published letters
and interviews.
The most celebrated scientist of the modern era believed that the most
beautiful emotion a human being could experience was the sense of the
mysterious. He called it the source of all true science and all true art.
A man of reason who never lost his sense of wonder –
which is why I also celebrate him as a true artist.

Siddhartha Gautama - the Buddha, fifth century BC.
He did not ask anyone to believe. He said: sit, watch, and see for
yourself. The most scientific instruction ever given by a spiritual
teacher. What he found at the edges of human consciousness, physicists
are only now beginning to sense at the edges of matter.

Various physicists - Quantum entanglement.
First demonstrated experimentally by Alain Aspect in 1982, building
on the theoretical work of Einstein, Podolsky and Rosen.
Two particles, once connected, remain connected across any distance.
Instantaneously. Without any visible mechanism. Einstein called it
spooky action at a distance and was deeply troubled by it.
He should not have been. It was simply the universe confirming what
the mystics had always known.

Plato - The Symposium, fourth century BC.
The oldest philosophical exploration of love as something that
transcends the personal - a condition of existence rather than an
emotion toward an object. Written two and a half thousand years ago.
Still unsurpassed.

www.ingramcontent.com/pod-product-compliance
Lightning Source LLC
Chambersburg PA
CBHW031358060726
47590CB00007B/2836